THE BOY PREFERRED ANIMALS TO PEOPLE.
<CHEEP CHEEP CHEEP CHU-REEP!>
1973
<CHEEP CHEEP CHEEP CHU-
PAP
IT'S OKAY. DR. JOSEPH IS HERE. ALL BETTER. FLY AWAY NOW.

Behind the Scenes: PETA's Tiger King Case Files

By Brittany Peet, PETA Foundation Deputy General Counsel for Captive Animal Law Enforcement

By the time I met "Joe Exotic," he'd been on PETA's radar for years. A PETA exposé revealed sick, injured, and dying animals at his facility. Animals were kicked, deprived of food, blasted with pressurized hoses and fire extinguishers, and beaten with the blunt end of a gun. We documented that operations like Joe's tear infant tiger cubs away from their mothers and then relegate them to cramped cages after they're too old to use as photo props. In response to our long-running campaign, Joe shot and hanged "PETA" in effigy and even threatened me by name on his show.

PETA eventually rescued almost 50 animals from his facility and got them placed in reputable sanctuaries—two of them were the chimpanzees featured at the end of Tiger King. They had lived in separate cages at Joe's roadside zoo for 10 years. When they were introduced during their first week at the sanctuary, they hugged for hours.

When I met Joe in 2017, he was falling out with Jeff Lowe and eager to give me the dirt on every tiger terrorizer he knew:

Jeff Lowe	**Tim Stark**	**"Doc" Antle**
Joe's business partner, who admitted to stuffing tiger cubs into suitcases and smuggling them into casinos	who acquired cubs from Joe, admitted to beating a leopard to death and declawing baby tigers. The	who acquired tiger cubs from Joe, according to him, sometimes kills those who've outgrown their usefulness in a gas chamber and then cremates them on site.

How You Can Help:

Never visit any business that offers hands-on interactions with wild animals. Visit PETA.org to learn more.

"THERE ARE RUMORS ABOUT YOUR MISSING HUSBAND AND YOU JUST SKIPPED OVER A BIG PORTION OF YOUR LIFE AND-"
"HE WENT MISSING IN 1992.
"YOU'VE BEEN WATCHING TOO MUCH NETFLIX OR READING TOO MANY MEMES.
"I DON'T HAVE ANYTHING ELSE TO SAY ABOUT IT. THERE'S AN INVESTIGATION."
THE GIRL FOUND A WAY TO WIN.

CPSIA information can be obtained
at www.ICGtesting.com
Printed in the USA
LVHW061021040720
659735LV00002B/43

9 781949 738544